Self-Compassion

Unlock the Power of Self-Love and Find Lasting Happiness:
A Guide to Cultivating Self-Compassion for a More Fulfilling Life

Lance P. Richards

I0625388

Self-Compassion: Unlock the Power of Self-Love and Find Lasting Happiness: A Guide to Cultivating Self-Compassion for a More Fulfilling Life

Table of Contents

01: Introduction: The Importance of Self-Compassion

Self-compassion is a simple yet powerful practice that can transform your life. It involves treating yourself with the same kindness, understanding, and support that you would offer to a dear friend who is going through a tough time. Self-compassion is not about self-pity, self-indulgence, or self-absorption. Rather, it is a way of relating to yourself that is grounded in self-awareness, self-acceptance, and self-love.

For many of us, the idea of being kind to ourselves can feel foreign or even uncomfortable. We may be more accustomed to criticizing ourselves for our perceived flaws, comparing ourselves to others, or setting impossibly high standards for ourselves. We may think that being hard on ourselves is necessary to motivate us to improve or succeed. However, research shows that self-criticism can actually undermine our well-being, making us more prone to anxiety, depression, and other forms of psychological distress.

Fortunately, self-compassion can help us break free from the cycle of self-criticism and find lasting happiness. By cultivating a compassionate attitude toward ourselves, we can

01: INTRODUCTION: THE IMPORTANCE OF SELF-COM-PASSION

learn to treat ourselves with the same care and understanding that we would extend to a close friend. This can help us feel more connected, supported, and empowered in our daily lives, and can foster greater resilience and emotional strength in the face of adversity.

In this book, we will explore the science of self-compassion, the benefits of this practice for our physical and mental health, and the steps we can take to cultivate self-compassion in our daily lives. We will examine the role of self-criticism in holding us back and explore how self-compassion can help us move forward. We will also delve into techniques for practicing self-compassion, such as meditation, breathing exercises, journaling, visualization, and gratitude.

Moreover, we will discuss how self-compassion can improve our relationships, our work, our creativity, and our spiritual well-being. We will look at the barriers that may prevent us from practicing self-compassion, and we will explore how we can overcome these barriers and maintain a self-compassionate attitude in the face of setbacks and challenges.

Overall, the goal of this book is to provide you with a comprehensive guide to cultivating self-compassion for a more

01: INTRODUCTION: THE IMPORTANCE OF SELF-COMPASSION

fulfilling life. Whether you are struggling with self-criticism, stress, anxiety, depression, or simply seeking greater happiness and well-being, this book can help you unlock the power of self-love and find lasting happiness through the practice of self-compassion.

02: Understanding Self-Compassion: What It Is and What It Isn't

Self-compassion is a term that is often used in popular media, but it is also a concept that is often misunderstood. In this chapter, we will explore what self-compassion is, what it isn't, and why it is so important for our well-being.

What Is Self-Compassion?

Self-compassion is a way of relating to ourselves that is grounded in kindness, understanding, and acceptance. It involves treating ourselves with the same care and concern that we would offer to a good friend. This means that we acknowledge our own suffering and pain, and we offer ourselves support and encouragement rather than criticism and judgment.

Self-compassion is made up of three components: self-kindness, common humanity, and mindfulness. Self-kindness involves treating ourselves with warmth and understanding, even when we make mistakes or experience difficult emotions. Common humanity involves recognizing that we are not alone in our struggles, and that all humans experience pain and suffering at some point in their lives. Mindfulness

involves being present and aware of our emotions and experiences, without judgment or avoidance.

What Self-Compassion Isn't

Self-compassion is often confused with self-pity, self-indulgence, or self-absorption. However, these attitudes are not
the same as self-compassion. Self-pity involves feeling sorry
for ourselves and seeking sympathy from others. Self-indulgence involves giving ourselves temporary pleasure or relief
without considering the long-term consequences. Self-absorption involves being overly focused on ourselves and our
own needs, to the exclusion of others.

Self-criticism is another attitude that is often confused with
self-compassion. While self-criticism may feel like a motiv-
ator for change, it can actually undermine our well-being
and make us less resilient in the face of challenges. Self-criticism involves being harsh and judgmental toward
ourselves when we make mistakes or experience difficult
emotions. This can lead to feelings of shame, anxiety, and
depression.

Why Is Self-Compassion Important?

02: UNDERSTANDING SELF-COMPASSION: WHAT IT IS AND WHAT IT ISN'T

Self-compassion is important for our physical and mental health, as well as our relationships and our work. Research has shown that self-compassion can improve our mood, reduce our levels of stress and anxiety, and increase our resilience in the face of adversity. It can also improve our relationships, by helping us feel more connected and empathetic toward others.

Self-compassion can also foster greater creativity and productivity in our work, by reducing our levels of stress and increasing our sense of self-worth. It can also help us be more innovative and flexible, by encouraging us to take risks and learn from our mistakes.

Moreover, self-compassion can lead to greater spiritual well-being, by helping us connect with our deepest values and sense of purpose. It can also help us cultivate a sense of gratitude and appreciation for the present moment, which can increase our overall sense of happiness and fulfillment in life.

Conclusion

In conclusion, self-compassion is a powerful practice that

can transform our lives in many ways. By learning to treat ourselves with kindness, understanding, and acceptance, we can find greater happiness, resilience, and fulfillment. It is not about self-pity, self-indulgence, or self-absorption, but rather about cultivating a compassionate attitude toward ourselves and others. In the next chapter, we will explore the benefits of self-compassion in more detail and examine the research behind this practice.

03: The Benefits of Self-Compassion for Your Physical and Mental Health

The Benefits of Self-Compassion for Your Physical and Mental Health

Self-compassion has been shown to have many positive effects on both our physical and mental health. In this chapter, we will explore the ways in which self-compassion can improve our well-being, and the research behind these benefits.

Physical Health Benefits of Self-Compassion

–Lower levels of stress

Research has found that self-compassion is associated with lower levels of the stress hormone cortisol. Cortisol is released in response to stress, and high levels of cortisol can have negative effects on our physical health, including an increased risk of heart disease, high blood pressure, and diabetes. By practicing self-compassion, we can reduce our stress levels and protect our physical health.

03: THE BENEFITS OF SELF-COMPASSION FOR YOUR PHYSICAL AND MENTAL HEALTH

– Better sleep

Self-compassion has also been linked to better sleep quality. This is likely due to the fact that self-compassion can reduce feelings of anxiety and stress, which can interfere with sleep. When we are kind and supportive toward ourselves, we are more likely to feel calm and relaxed, which can lead to better sleep.

– Reduced pain and inflammation

Research has found that self-compassion can help reduce pain and inflammation in the body. This is because self-compassion can reduce feelings of stress, which can exacerbate pain and inflammation. By practicing self-compassion, we can help our bodies heal and reduce physical discomfort.

Mental Health Benefits of Self-Compassion

– Reduced anxiety and depression

Self-compassion has been shown to be an effective tool for reducing symptoms of anxiety and depression. When we are kind and understanding toward ourselves, we are less likely to experience negative self-talk, self-doubt, and self-criticism, which can contribute to feelings of anxiety and depression.

– Increased resilience

Self-compassion can also increase our resilience in the face of challenges and setbacks. When we are kind and supportive toward ourselves, we are better able to bounce back from difficult situations and maintain a positive outlook on life. This can help us feel more in control of our lives, even when things don't go as planned.

– Improved self-esteem

By practicing self-compassion, we can also improve our self-esteem. When we are kind and accepting toward ourselves, we are more likely to feel good about who we are and what we have to offer. This can help us feel more confident in our relationships, our work, and our daily lives.

– Greater emotional regulation

Self-compassion can also improve our ability to regulate our emotions. When we are kind and supportive toward ourselves, we are better able to manage difficult emotions like anger, sadness, and anxiety. This can help us avoid emotional outbursts and make more rational decisions, even when we are feeling overwhelmed.

Conclusion

In conclusion, self-compassion has many physical and mental health benefits. By practicing self-compassion, we can reduce our stress levels, improve our sleep quality, reduce pain and inflammation, reduce symptoms of anxiety and depression, increase our resilience, improve our self-esteem, and improve our ability to regulate our emotions. These benefits can lead to a more fulfilling and satisfying life, with greater happiness, productivity, and overall well-being. In the next chapter, we will explore how to cultivate self-compassion in our daily lives.

04: The Science of Self-Compassion: Research and Evidence

Over the past few decades, there has been a growing interest in the science of self-compassion. Researchers have conducted numerous studies on the benefits of self-compassion, as well as the factors that contribute to its development. In this chapter, we will explore the research and evidence behind self-compassion.

Defining Self-Compassion

Self-compassion is defined as treating oneself with kindness, understanding, and acceptance, especially during difficult times. It involves recognizing that suffering is a normal part of the human experience, and responding to our own suffering with compassion rather than self-criticism or judgment.

Research on Self-Compassion

– Benefits of Self-Compassion

Numerous studies have found that self-compassion is associated with many positive outcomes, including reduced levels of anxiety and depression, improved emotional regulation, increased life satisfaction, and improved physical health.

For example, a study published in the Journal of Personality and Social Psychology found that self-compassion was associated with lower levels of anxiety and depression, even when controlling for factors like self-esteem and coping styles. Another study published in the Journal of Health Psychology found that self-compassion was associated with greater happiness and life satisfaction.

– Development of Self-Compassion

Research has also explored the factors that contribute to the development of self-compassion. Some studies have found that self-compassion is related to certain personality traits, such as openness and conscientiousness. Other studies have found that mindfulness and self-compassion practices, such as meditation and self-compassionate letter writing, can increase self-compassion over time.

For example, a study published in the Journal of Positive Psychology found that a self-compassion meditation practice increased participants' levels of self-compassion over a four-week period. Another study published in the Journal of Clinical Psychology found that a self-compassionate letter writing intervention improved participants' self-compassion and reduced their symptoms of depression.

– Cultural Differences in Self-Compassion

Research has also explored cultural differences in self-compassion. Some studies have found that people from collectivistic cultures, such as Asian cultures, may have lower levels of self-compassion compared to people from individualistic cultures, such as Western cultures. This may be due to cultural values that prioritize self-criticism and self-improvement over self-compassion and self-acceptance.

Implications for Practice

The research on self-compassion has important implications for how we can cultivate self-compassion in our daily lives. Some strategies that have been found to be effective include:

– Practicing mindfulness and self-compassion meditations

– Writing self-compassionate letters to ourselves

– Identifying and challenging self-critical thoughts and beliefs

– Practicing self-care and self-nurturing behaviors

By incorporating these practices into our daily lives, we can increase our levels of self-compassion and experience the many benefits that come with it.

Conclusion

In conclusion, the research on self-compassion has demonstrated that it is a valuable tool for improving our physical and mental health, increasing our resilience, and improving our overall well-being. The development of self-compassion can be facilitated through mindfulness and self-compassion practices, and by identifying and challenging self-critical thoughts and beliefs. By cultivating self-compassion, we can improve our relationship with ourselves and experience greater happiness, fulfillment, and success in our lives.

05: How Self-Criticism Can Hold You Back and How Self-Compassion Can Help You Move Forward

Self-criticism is a common tendency for many people. We often hold ourselves to impossibly high standards and become our own harshest critics when we inevitably fall short. While some degree of self-evaluation and self-correction can be healthy and motivating, constant self-criticism can become a roadblock to our personal growth and happiness.

In this chapter, we will explore the ways that self-criticism can hold us back, and how cultivating self-compassion can help us move forward.

Self-Criticism: The Roadblock to Growth

Self-criticism can be a self-fulfilling prophecy. When we are constantly critical of ourselves, we can become stuck in a cycle of negative self-talk, which can lead to anxiety, depression, and feelings of worthlessness. It can be difficult to see a way out of this cycle, as the negative thoughts can feel overwhelming and all-encompassing.

Additionally, self-criticism can also lead to a fear of failure.

05: HOW SELF-CRITICISM CAN HOLD YOU BACK AND HOW SELF-COMPASSION CAN HELP YOU MOVE FORWARD

When we are overly critical of ourselves, we may become paralyzed by the fear of making mistakes, and as a result, we may avoid taking risks or trying new things. This can prevent us from reaching our full potential and experiencing personal growth.

Self-Compassion: The Path to Healing

The good news is that self-compassion can provide a path out of the cycle of self-criticism. By treating ourselves with kindness and understanding, we can break free from the negative self-talk and cultivate a healthier mindset.

Self-compassion involves three key components: self-kindness, common humanity, and mindfulness. Self-kindness means treating ourselves with the same level of care and concern that we would offer to a friend who is struggling. Common humanity involves recognizing that suffering is a part of the human experience, and that we are not alone in our struggles. Finally, mindfulness means being present and aware of our thoughts and feelings, without judgment.

Practicing Self-Compassion

05: HOW SELF-CRITICISM CAN HOLD YOU BACK AND HOW SELF-COMPASSION CAN HELP YOU MOVE FORWARD

There are several strategies and techniques that can help us cultivate self-compassion in our daily lives. Here are a few to consider:

– Notice and label self-critical thoughts: When we become aware of our negative self-talk, we can start to challenge and reframe these thoughts. Try writing down your self-critical thoughts and then writing compassionate and supportive responses to them.

– Practice self-care: Taking care of ourselves physically and emotionally can be a powerful act of self-compassion. Make time for activities that you enjoy, prioritize rest and relaxation, and seek out support from friends and family.

– Practice self-compassion meditation: This type of meditation involves directing kind and supportive thoughts towards ourselves. There are many guided self-compassion meditations available online, or you can try creating your own script.

– Cultivate a growth mindset: Instead of viewing mistakes and failures as evidence of personal flaws, try to reframe them as opportunities for growth and learning. When we approach challenges with a growth mindset, we can become more resilient and open to new experiences.

Conclusion

Self-criticism can be a roadblock to personal growth and happiness, but cultivating self-compassion can provide a path forward. By treating ourselves with kindness and understanding, we can break free from negative self-talk and start to view ourselves with greater compassion and self-love.

06: The Link Between Self-Compassion and Emotional Resilience

The world we live in is full of uncertainties, which means that life can throw curveballs at us at any time. These unexpected changes can have a significant impact on our emotional well-being, and they can cause a great deal of stress, anxiety, and even depression.

However, research shows that individuals who practice self-compassion are better equipped to handle these types of situations, and they are more emotionally resilient in the face of adversity.

So, what is emotional resilience, and how does it relate to self-compassion?

Emotional resilience is the ability to adapt to life's challenges and bounce back from difficult experiences. When we face a challenge, emotional resilience helps us manage our emotions, maintain a positive outlook, and cope with the stress that comes with change.

Self-compassion is closely related to emotional resilience because it helps us regulate our emotions and build a sense of inner strength. It allows us to view ourselves in a positive light, even when we make mistakes or experience failure. It encourages us to treat ourselves with kindness and understanding, which helps us build the emotional resilience necessary to face life's challenges.

A study published in the Journal of Positive Psychology examined the relationship between self-compassion and emotional resilience. The study found that individuals who practice self-compassion were better able to cope with negative emotions, such as anxiety and depression, and they were more likely to recover from difficult experiences.

The study also found that self-compassion was positively associated with well-being and happiness, suggesting that cultivating self-compassion is not just important for building emotional resilience but also for promoting overall mental health.

Another study published in the Journal of Happiness Studies examined the relationship between self-compassion and resilience in a group of college students. The study found that students who reported higher levels of self-compassion were better able to cope with academic stress, and they had a greater sense of resilience overall.

These studies suggest that practicing self-compassion can be a powerful tool for building emotional resilience and coping with life's challenges. By treating ourselves with kindness and understanding, we can build the inner strength necessary to face adversity and maintain a positive outlook on life.

So, how can we cultivate self-compassion to build emotional resilience?

One way is to practice self-compassion meditation, which involves directing kind and supportive thoughts towards ourselves. We can also practice self-care by engaging in activities that promote our physical and emotional well-being, such as exercise, meditation, and spending time with loved ones.

Finally, we can work to reframe our negative self-talk into more positive and compassionate self-talk. When we make mistakes, we can acknowledge our shortcomings without beating ourselves up, and instead, focus on how we can learn and grow from the experience.

06: THE LINK BETWEEN SELF-COMPASSION AND EMOTIONAL RESILIENCE

In conclusion, self-compassion is closely related to emotional resilience, and cultivating self-compassion can help us build the inner strength necessary to face life's challenges. By practicing self-compassion, we can regulate our emotions, maintain a positive outlook, and cope with stress and adversity, which can ultimately lead to greater well-being and happiness.

07: Recognizing and Acknowledging Your Suffering

Self-compassion is all about treating ourselves with the same kindness and concern that we would offer to a good friend who is suffering. It is about being aware of our own struggles and pains and approaching them with understanding, warmth, and acceptance. However, before we can extend self-compassion to ourselves, we need to be able to recognize and acknowledge our suffering.

Many people find it difficult to acknowledge their own pain, either because they think it makes them weak, they don't want to burden others, or they simply don't know how to do it. But avoiding or denying our suffering only makes things worse. We end up feeling more isolated, disconnected, and overwhelmed, which can lead to anxiety, depression, and other mental health issues.

Recognizing our suffering is the first step in cultivating self-compassion. It means acknowledging that something is causing us pain, and being willing to give it our attention and care. Here are some steps you can take to recognize and acknowledge your suffering:

07: RECOGNIZING AND ACKNOWLEDGING YOUR SUFFERING

– Pay attention to your thoughts and feelings. One of the easiest ways to recognize your suffering is to simply pay attention to your thoughts and feelings. Notice when you're feeling stressed, anxious, sad, or angry. Pay attention to the thoughts that are going through your mind, and try to identify any negative or self-critical patterns.

– Validate your feelings. Once you've recognized your suffering, it's important to validate your feelings. This means acknowledging that your pain is real, and that it's okay to feel the way you do. Sometimes we try to minimize our suffering, or compare it to others who may be going through worse. However, this only invalidates our own feelings and makes it harder to heal.

– Identify the source of your suffering. Once you've validated your feelings, try to identify the source of your suffering. Is it a relationship problem? Work stress? Health issues? Identifying the source of your suffering can help you understand it better and take steps to address it.

– Talk to someone you trust. Sharing your suffering with someone you trust can be a powerful way to acknowledge and validate your feelings. It can also help you gain perspective, and receive support and encouragement. Choose someone who you feel comfortable talking to, and who will listen without judgment.

– Practice mindfulness. Mindfulness is a powerful tool for recognizing and acknowledging your suffering. It involves paying attention to the present moment, without judgment or distraction. By being present with your thoughts and feelings, you can become more aware of your suffering and learn to accept it with kindness and compassion.

Recognizing and acknowledging your suffering is not always easy, but it is an essential step in cultivating self-compassion. When we're able to recognize our own pain and treat it with understanding and kindness, we open ourselves up to greater healing and growth.

08: Accepting Yourself as You Are

Accepting yourself as you are is a critical aspect of self-compassion. It involves recognizing your strengths, weaknesses, and limitations and embracing them with kindness, rather than criticism. Unfortunately, many of us struggle with self-acceptance, and instead, we spend a significant amount of time and energy trying to be someone else or conforming to societal expectations.

Self-acceptance is not about ignoring your flaws or denying areas where you need to improve; it's about recognizing your humanness and being kind to yourself. It's about treating yourself with the same kindness, care, and understanding that you would extend to a friend who is going through a difficult time.

It's common to believe that accepting yourself means that you are settling for less or that you're not striving for improvement. However, self-acceptance is not about giving up on your goals or ambitions. It's about starting from a place of kindness and compassion, where you acknowledge your efforts and progress and recognize that setbacks and failures are a natural part of the journey.

Self-acceptance begins with cultivating self-awareness. By

acknowledging your thoughts, feelings, and actions, you can identify patterns and behaviors that may be holding you back from accepting yourself. One effective way to increase self-awareness is through mindfulness practices. Mindfulness involves paying attention to the present moment with curiosity and without judgment. This approach can help you to observe your thoughts and feelings and allow them to pass without getting caught up in them.

Another way to increase self-acceptance is to focus on your strengths and positive attributes. We often focus on our flaws and shortcomings, but by intentionally looking for our strengths, we can shift our mindset and begin to accept ourselves more fully. One useful technique is to make a list of your positive qualities and read them regularly, reminding yourself of what you have to offer the world.

Another important aspect of self-acceptance is releasing the need for external validation. We often seek approval and acceptance from others, but this can be an exhausting and unfulfilling pursuit. Instead, we need to focus on validating ourselves and recognizing our own worth. One way to do this is to practice self-compassion, as it helps to cultivate a sense of self-worth and a belief in our own value.

Finally, self-acceptance is an ongoing journey, not a destination. We are constantly growing and changing, and so our ability to accept ourselves needs to evolve as well. By committing to a practice of self-compassion and self-awareness, we can continue to grow in our self-acceptance and find greater peace and fulfillment in our lives.

09: Letting Go of Perfectionism and Embracing Imperfection

Perfectionism is a common trait among many people, and it can lead to intense feelings of anxiety, stress, and self-criticism. While striving for excellence can be a positive quality, perfectionism takes it to an extreme that can be detrimental to one's mental and emotional well-being. This is where self-compassion comes in, as it can help you let go of perfectionism and embrace your imperfections.

Perfectionism is often driven by a fear of failure or a desire to meet impossible standards. It can lead to a constant feeling of never being good enough and can create a cycle of self-criticism and negative self-talk. When you are caught in this cycle, it can be difficult to see yourself as anything other than your flaws and shortcomings. This is where self-compassion can help. By showing yourself kindness and understanding, you can break free from the cycle of perfectionism and learn to accept yourself as you are.

One of the key aspects of self-compassion is recognizing that everyone is imperfect, and that is okay. It is essential to let go of the belief that you have to be perfect in order to be worthy or successful. Instead, focus on being kind to yourself and understanding that making mistakes is a natural part of the learning process. By embracing your imperfections, you can learn to see them as opportunities for growth rather than as reasons to criticize yourself.

Another important part of letting go of perfectionism is learning to set realistic goals and expectations for yourself. This means accepting that you may not always get everything right the first time, and that it's okay to make mistakes. Instead of striving for perfection, focus on making progress and celebrating your accomplishments along the way. By setting achievable goals and acknowledging your progress, you can build confidence and self-esteem while also reducing the pressure to be perfect.

Self-compassion can also help you overcome the fear of failure that often accompanies perfectionism. When you are self-compassionate, you can acknowledge that failure is a natural part of the learning process, and that it does not define your worth as a person. This can help you take risks and try new things without the fear of making mistakes or failing.

In addition to these practical strategies, it's important to

09: LETTING GO OF PERFECTIONISM AND EMBRA-CING IMPERFECTION

cultivate a mindset of self-acceptance and self-compassion. This means learning to treat yourself with the same kindness and understanding that you would show to a friend or loved one. When you make a mistake, instead of beating yourself up, try to offer yourself words of encouragement and support. By treating yourself with compassion and understanding, you can learn to love and accept yourself as you are, imperfections and all.

In conclusion, letting go of perfectionism and embracing imperfection is an important part of cultivating self-compassion. By acknowledging that everyone is imperfect and that making mistakes is a natural part of the learning process, you can break free from the cycle of self-criticism and negative self-talk. By setting realistic goals, taking risks, and treating yourself with kindness and understanding, you can learn to accept yourself as you are and embrace your imperfections as opportunities for growth and learning.

10: Developing Self-Kindness: Treating Yourself with Care and Understanding

As you embark on the journey of cultivating self-compassion, one of the most crucial components to focus on is developing self-kindness. Treating yourself with care and understanding is essential if you want to build a healthy relationship with yourself and cultivate a more fulfilling life.

Many of us are our own worst critics, and we often hold ourselves to high standards that are impossible to meet. We are quick to judge and criticize ourselves for our flaws, mistakes, and failures. We beat ourselves up for not being perfect, and we set impossibly high expectations for ourselves.

But when we treat ourselves with kindness and understanding, we create an environment of support, encouragement, and love that can help us thrive. Self-kindness means treating ourselves like we would treat a dear friend or loved one. It means acknowledging our mistakes and failures with compassion and understanding and recognizing our strengths and accomplishments.

So, how do you start to develop self-kindness? Here are

some tips to get you started:

– Practice Self-Care: Taking care of yourself is an essential part of treating yourself with kindness. Make time for activities that nourish your body, mind, and soul. This can include things like exercise, meditation, spending time in nature, reading, or practicing a hobby.

– Practice Self-Compassion: Self-compassion is the act of treating yourself with kindness and understanding in the face of difficult emotions or experiences. Instead of beating yourself up for your mistakes or failures, practice self-compassion by offering yourself words of support and encouragement.

– Practice Positive Self-Talk: Pay attention to the way you talk to yourself. Are you constantly criticizing and judging yourself? If so, try to shift your focus to positive self-talk. Talk to yourself like you would talk to a friend, offering words of encouragement and support.

– Practice Gratitude: Focus on the positive things in your life and express gratitude for them. Cultivating a sense of gratitude can help shift your perspective from negative to positive and help you feel more connected to the good things in your life.

– Practice Forgiveness: Forgiveness is a powerful tool for cultivating self-kindness. Let go of grudges and resentments and offer yourself and others forgiveness. Remember that forgiveness is not about condoning bad behavior, but about releasing yourself from the negative emotions that can hold you back.

Developing self-kindness takes time and practice, but the benefits are worth it. By treating yourself with care and understanding, you can create a more loving and supportive relationship with yourself that can help you achieve your goals and lead a more fulfilling life. So, be kind to yourself, and remember that you are worthy of love and compassion.

11: Practicing Self-Compassion in Challenging Moments

In the previous chapter, we discussed the importance of developing self-kindness and how it can lead to a more fulfilling life. In this chapter, we'll delve into the practical ways to apply self-compassion in challenging moments.

One of the most important things to understand about self-compassion is that it's not about trying to eliminate difficult emotions or pretending that everything is fine when it's not. Instead, it's about acknowledging that you're struggling and offering yourself the same kind of support and understanding that you would offer to a friend.

Here are some strategies for practicing self-compassion in challenging moments:

– Mindful Awareness: Mindfulness is a key component of self-compassion. When you're faced with a difficult situation or emotion, try to observe it without judgment. Instead of immediately reacting, take a moment to pause and notice what you're feeling. This can help you gain a better understanding of your emotions and respond more skillfully.

11: PRACTICING SELF-COMPASSION IN CHALLENGING MOMENTS

– Self-Talk: The way you talk to yourself can have a big impact on how you feel. When you're facing a challenging moment, try to use kind and supportive language with yourself. For example, instead of saying "I can't do this," try saying "This is really hard, but I'm doing my best." This can help you feel more motivated and less overwhelmed.

– Self-Soothing: When you're feeling stressed or anxious, it can be helpful to engage in activities that make you feel calm and comfortable. This might include taking a warm bath, listening to music, or cuddling with a pet. These small acts of self-care can help you feel more grounded and resilient.

– Perspective-Taking: Sometimes, it can be helpful to put your problems in perspective. When you're feeling overwhelmed, try to think about the bigger picture. Will this matter in a year? Will it matter in five years? This can help you see that the problem is temporary and that you're capable of handling it.

– Embracing Common Humanity: Remember that you're not alone in your struggles. Everyone experiences difficult emotions and challenging moments. By acknowledging this, you can feel more connected to others and less isolated in your suffering.

– Practice Gratitude: Gratitude can be a powerful antidote to negative emotions. When you're feeling down, try to focus on the things in your life that you're grateful for. This can help you feel more positive and hopeful.

– Reframe Failure: Failure is a natural part of the learning process. Instead of beating yourself up for your mistakes, try to reframe them as opportunities for growth. What can you learn from this experience? How can you use this knowledge to improve in the future?

Practicing self-compassion in challenging moments takes time and effort. It's important to remember that self-compassion is a skill that can be developed with practice. Be patient with yourself and remember that every small act of self-compassion can have a positive impact on your well-being.

12: Transforming Negative Self-Talk into Positive Self-Talk

Negative self-talk can be one of the most damaging things we do to ourselves. It's the voice in our head that tells us we're not good enough, smart enough, pretty enough, or worthy enough. This negative self-talk can cause us to feel anxious, depressed, and can even lead to physical health problems.

Fortunately, we can learn to transform our negative self-talk into positive self-talk. With self-compassion, we can learn to treat ourselves with kindness and understanding, even in difficult moments.

Here are some steps to transforming negative self-talk into positive self-talk:

– Recognize negative self-talk: The first step in transforming negative self-talk is to recognize when it's happening. You might notice it when you're feeling anxious, stressed, or upset. Pay attention to the thoughts that are going through your mind and notice if they're negative or critical.

– Challenge negative self-talk: Once you've recognized negative self-talk, challenge it. Ask yourself if what you're thinking is really true. Is there evidence to support it? Would you say the same thing to a friend who was in the same situation?

– Reframe negative self-talk: Reframing negative self-talk means turning it into something positive. For example, if you're thinking "I can't do this," reframe it as "I may not be able to do this yet, but I can learn and improve."

– Practice self-compassion: Practicing self-compassion means treating yourself with kindness and understanding. This involves acknowledging that it's okay to make mistakes and that everyone has flaws. Treat yourself like you would treat a friend who was struggling.

– Use positive affirmations: Positive affirmations are statements that you repeat to yourself to promote positive thinking and self-compassion. For example, you might say "I am enough" or "I am worthy of love and acceptance."

– Celebrate small successes: Celebrating small successes can help build confidence and self-esteem. When you achieve something, no matter how small, take a moment to acknowledge it and feel proud of yourself.

– Surround yourself with positivity: Surround yourself with positive people and positive messages. Read books or listen to podcasts that promote self-compassion and positivity.

In summary, transforming negative self-talk into positive self-talk is an important aspect of cultivating self-compassion. By recognizing negative self-talk, challenging it, reframing it, practicing self-compassion, using positive affirmations, celebrating small successes, and surrounding yourself with positivity, you can learn to treat yourself with kindness and understanding, even in challenging moments.

13: Nurturing a Mindful Attitude and Presence

Introduction:

One of the fundamental elements of self-compassion is mindfulness. Mindfulness is the practice of being fully present and engaged in the current moment, observing our thoughts, feelings, and sensations without judgment. When we practice mindfulness, we become more aware of our mental and emotional processes, which helps us develop a more compassionate relationship with ourselves. In this chapter, we will explore the concept of mindfulness, how it relates to self-compassion, and how to cultivate a more mindful attitude in our daily lives.

What is Mindfulness?

Mindfulness is an ancient practice that has its roots in Buddhist meditation. The basic idea is to pay attention to the present moment without judgment. This means noticing your thoughts, feelings, and sensations as they arise, but not getting caught up in them or trying to change them. Mindfulness involves being fully present and engaged in the current moment, without being distracted by worries about the future or regrets about the past.

How Does Mindfulness Relate to Self-Compassion?

Practicing mindfulness can help us develop self-compassion in several ways. First, mindfulness helps us become more aware of our thoughts and feelings, including negative self-talk and self-criticism. By observing these thoughts without judgment, we can learn to identify them as simply thoughts, rather than objective truths. This allows us to create distance from these thoughts and respond to them with more compassion.

Second, mindfulness helps us develop a more accepting and non-judgmental attitude towards ourselves. When we practice mindfulness, we learn to observe our thoughts and feelings with curiosity and openness, rather than judgment or criticism. This attitude of openness and curiosity can help us cultivate self-compassion and kindness towards ourselves, even when we are experiencing difficult emotions or challenging situations.

Cultivating a Mindful Attitude

13: NURTURING A MINDFUL ATTITUDE AND PRESENCE

Developing a mindful attitude takes practice, but it is a skill that anyone can learn. Here are some tips for cultivating a more mindful attitude:

– Practice mindfulness meditation: Mindfulness meditation is a practice that involves sitting in a quiet place and focusing on your breath. When your mind wanders, you simply notice it and gently bring your attention back to your breath. This practice can help you become more aware of your thoughts and feelings, and develop a more accepting attitude towards them.

– Practice mindfulness throughout the day: You don't need to set aside time for formal meditation to practice mindfulness. You can practice mindfulness throughout the day by simply paying attention to your thoughts, feelings, and sensations as they arise. When you notice negative self-talk or self-criticism, try to observe these thoughts with curiosity and openness, rather than judgment or criticism.

– Take a mindful approach to everyday activities: You can practice mindfulness while doing everyday activities, such as washing dishes or walking the dog. Simply focus on the sensations and experiences of the activity, rather than allowing your mind to wander to other thoughts or distractions.

– Practice self-compassion: Remember that mindfulness is just one element of self-compassion. As you practice mindfulness, try to bring a sense of kindness and compassion to your thoughts and feelings, even when they are difficult or uncomfortable. Remember that self-compassion involves treating yourself with care and understanding, even when you make mistakes or face challenges.

Conclusion:

Cultivating a more mindful attitude is a key component of developing self-compassion. By practicing mindfulness, we can become more aware of our thoughts and feelings, develop a more accepting attitude towards ourselves, and respond to difficult emotions with greater kindness and compassion. With practice and patience, anyone can develop a more mindful attitude and experience the many benefits of self-compassion in their daily lives.

14: Overcoming Self-Judgment and Self-Doubt

Introduction:

Self-judgment and self-doubt are common experiences for many people. We are often our own harshest critics, and we can be quick to doubt our own abilities, worth, and potential. These patterns of thinking can be incredibly damaging to our sense of self and our ability to reach our goals and live fulfilling lives. However, through the practice of self-compassion, we can begin to overcome these negative thought patterns and learn to treat ourselves with greater kindness and understanding.

Understanding Self-Judgment and Self-Doubt:

Self-judgment and self-doubt are two sides of the same coin. When we judge ourselves harshly, we are often doing so out of a sense of self-doubt. We may feel like we are not good enough, that we don't measure up to others, or that we are somehow flawed or defective. This can lead us to be overly critical of ourselves, to constantly compare ourselves to others, and to feel like we are not deserving of love, success, or happiness.

14: OVERCOMING SELF-JUDGMENT AND SELF-DOUBT

Self-doubt can be incredibly insidious, as it often operates in the background of our minds, shaping our thoughts and actions without our even realizing it. It can prevent us from taking risks, trying new things, and pursuing our goals. It can also cause us to second-guess ourselves and our decisions, leading to a lack of confidence and a sense of feeling stuck.

Overcoming Self-Judgment and Self-Doubt with Self-Compassion:

Self-compassion can be a powerful antidote to self-judgment and self-doubt. When we practice self-compassion, we learn to treat ourselves with greater kindness and understanding, recognizing that we are all human and that making mistakes and struggling are a normal part of the human experience.

One of the key aspects of self-compassion is learning to observe our thoughts and emotions without judgment. When we become aware of our negative self-talk, we can begin to challenge those thoughts and replace them with more positive and affirming ones. This can be a difficult practice at first, as our negative thoughts may feel automatic and deeply ingrained. However, with time and practice, we can begin to rewire our brains and develop more positive and self-affirming thought patterns.

Another important aspect of self-compassion is learning to be present with our emotions and feelings, rather than trying to suppress or ignore them. When we are able to acknowledge and validate our own emotions, we can begin to process them in a more healthy and productive way. This can help to reduce our sense of self-doubt and anxiety, as we become more comfortable with the ebb and flow of our emotions.

Practicing self-compassion can also help us to develop greater resilience and a more positive outlook on life. When we are kinder to ourselves, we are better able to bounce back from setbacks and challenges, and to approach life with a sense of curiosity and openness. This can help us to cultivate a greater sense of self-trust and confidence, allowing us to pursue our goals and dreams with greater ease and grace.

Conclusion:

Self-judgment and self-doubt can be incredibly challenging

experiences, but they are not insurmountable. Through the practice of self-compassion, we can learn to treat ourselves with greater kindness and understanding, and to overcome our negative thought patterns. This can help us to live more fulfilling and meaningful lives, and to realize our full potential as human beings.

15: Embracing Your Emotions with Kindness and Curiosity

Emotions are a vital part of the human experience, and they play a significant role in how we perceive and interact with the world around us. While emotions can be a source of great joy and connection, they can also be a source of discomfort, pain, and suffering. For many of us, emotions can be challenging to manage, and we may feel overwhelmed, powerless, or confused when we experience them.

One of the keys to cultivating self-compassion is learning to embrace your emotions with kindness and curiosity. Self-compassion involves accepting your emotions, even the difficult ones, and treating yourself with kindness and understanding. This can help you develop a more positive relationship with your emotions, and transform the way you respond to them.

The first step to embracing your emotions with kindness and curiosity is to become more aware of them. Many of us tend to ignore or suppress our emotions, especially the negative ones, which can lead to feelings of tension, anxiety, and disconnection. Mindfulness can be an excellent tool for becoming more aware of your emotions, as it allows you to observe them with curiosity and without judgment.

When you experience an emotion, try to acknowledge it and identify it. For example, if you are feeling sad, you might say to yourself, "I am feeling sad right now." This simple act of labeling can help you connect with your emotions and make them feel less overwhelming.

Once you have identified your emotions, you can begin to explore them with curiosity. Ask yourself questions like, "What triggered this emotion?" or "What is this emotion trying to tell me?" By examining your emotions with curiosity, you can gain insights into your inner world and better understand what drives your feelings and behaviors.

Another critical component of embracing your emotions with kindness and curiosity is learning to respond to them in a self-compassionate way. When you experience a difficult emotion, it's natural to want to push it away or distract yourself from it. However, this approach can backfire, as it may lead to more significant emotional distress in the long run.

Instead of avoiding your emotions, try to respond to them

with kindness and understanding. This can involve offering yourself words of comfort, such as "It's okay to feel this way" or "I'm here for you." You might also try placing a hand on your heart or stomach as a physical reminder of your intention to offer yourself compassion.

Remember that your emotions are not good or bad; they are merely information about your internal experience. By learning to embrace your emotions with kindness and curiosity, you can develop a more positive relationship with them and use them as a source of insight and growth.

In conclusion, embracing your emotions with kindness and curiosity is an essential part of cultivating self-compassion. By becoming more aware of your emotions, exploring them with curiosity, and responding to them with kindness and understanding, you can transform the way you relate to your internal world. With practice, you can learn to view your emotions as allies rather than enemies, and use them to guide you towards a more fulfilling and compassionate life.

16: Developing a Self-Compassionate Inner Dialogue

As human beings, we engage in self-talk throughout our lives, and the nature of our self-talk can have a profound impact on our emotional well-being. The way we talk to ourselves in difficult or challenging moments can either build us up or tear us down. Many people are not aware of the power of their self-talk, and it can often be critical, negative, and unkind. This is where self-compassion comes in. Practicing self-compassion can help you develop a more self-compassionate inner dialogue that can significantly improve your emotional well-being and lead to greater self-acceptance.

One of the key components of self-compassion is self-kindness, which involves treating yourself with warmth, care, and understanding. When you encounter a challenging situation, you might typically respond with self-criticism, telling yourself things like, "I'm such an idiot," "I always mess things up," or "I can't do anything right." However, with self-compassion, you can learn to respond with self-kindness instead. This means speaking to yourself as you would to a good friend who was going through a tough time. You might say something like, "It's okay, I'm doing the best I can," or "I'm still learning, and that's okay."

Another important component of developing a self-compassionate inner dialogue is mindfulness. Mindfulness is the practice of being present and fully engaged in the current moment, without judgment. When you're experiencing difficult emotions, practicing mindfulness can help you stay present with those emotions without getting caught up in negative thoughts or judgments. Mindfulness can also help you become more aware of your self-talk and the ways in which you talk to yourself, allowing you to make conscious choices about how you respond to your emotions and thoughts.

One practical technique for developing a more self-compassionate inner dialogue is the practice of cognitive restructuring. Cognitive restructuring involves identifying negative thoughts and beliefs and replacing them with more positive and self-compassionate ones. For example, if you're struggling with feelings of inadequacy, you might identify negative self-talk like, "I'm not good enough," or "I'll never measure up." You can then challenge those thoughts by asking yourself questions like, "Is that really true?" or "What evidence do I have that I'm not good enough?" Once you've identified and challenged those negative thoughts, you can replace them with more positive and self-compassionate ones, like "I'm doing the best I can," or "I'm enough just as I am."

Another helpful technique is the use of self-compassionate imagery. Self-compassionate imagery involves imagining a kind and compassionate presence, such as a mentor, friend, or spiritual figure, who can offer you support and encouragement in difficult moments. You might imagine this person holding your hand or offering you a gentle hug, while speaking words of kindness and encouragement. This can help you access feelings of warmth and kindness towards yourself, and can also help you cultivate a more self-compassionate inner dialogue.

In order to develop a more self-compassionate inner dialogue, it's also important to be patient and gentle with yourself. Changing old patterns of negative self-talk can take time and practice, and it's important to be patient and forgiving with yourself as you learn and grow. When you notice that you're engaging in self-criticism, remind yourself that it's okay to make mistakes and that you're still learning. With practice, you can develop a more self-compassionate inner dialogue that can help you feel more confident, resilient, and at peace with yourself.

17: Learning to Forgive Yourself and Others

Forgiveness is often seen as an act of kindness towards others, but it is equally important to extend this same compassion to oneself. Forgiving oneself is an essential aspect of self-compassion that allows individuals to move past past mistakes and missteps, and to focus on growth and self-improvement.

Forgiving oneself is often difficult due to the self-judgment and negative self-talk that is frequently present in one's own internal dialogue. Many people tend to be overly harsh and critical of themselves, often holding themselves to impossibly high standards that they are unable to meet. This can lead to feelings of shame, guilt, and inadequacy, and can be a significant obstacle to practicing self-compassion.

To begin the process of forgiving oneself, it is important to first recognize and acknowledge any negative self-talk and self-judgment that is present. This can involve bringing awareness to one's own internal dialogue, and actively working to reframe negative self-talk in a more positive light. For example, instead of saying "I'm so stupid for making that mistake," one might reframe that statement to

17: LEARNING TO FORGIVE YOURSELF AND OTHERS

"Everyone makes mistakes, and I can learn from this experience to do better next time."

Another important aspect of forgiving oneself is to acknowledge and accept the emotions that come with mistakes and missteps. It is normal to feel guilt, shame, or regret when something goes wrong, but it is important to remember that these emotions do not define us as individuals. By accepting and embracing these emotions, individuals can begin to let go of the negative self-talk and judgments that can hold them back.

Forgiving oneself also involves taking responsibility for one's actions and making amends as needed. This can involve apologizing to others who may have been affected by one's actions, and actively working to make things right. It is important to remember, however, that self-forgiveness is not about absolving oneself of responsibility, but rather about acknowledging the mistake and taking steps to make things right.

It is also important to remember that forgiveness is a process, and it may take time to fully let go of negative emotions and self-judgment. Practicing self-compassion can help to support this process, by providing a safe and nurturing environment to acknowledge and work through difficult emotions.

Finally, forgiveness is not just about forgiving oneself, but also about extending forgiveness to others. Holding onto grudges and resentments can be a significant barrier to self-compassion, as it can lead to feelings of anger and frustration that can be directed inward. By practicing forgiveness towards others, individuals can free themselves from these negative emotions and create a more positive and compassionate internal dialogue.

In summary, learning to forgive oneself is an essential aspect of cultivating self-compassion. It involves acknowledging and accepting one's mistakes and missteps, reframing negative self-talk, and taking responsibility for one's actions. It is a process that takes time and patience, but it is an important step towards creating a more positive and compassionate relationship with oneself. By extending forgiveness to oneself and others, individuals can create a more nurturing and supportive internal dialogue, and move towards a more fulfilling and compassionate life.

18: Exploring and Understanding the Roots of Self-Criticism

In order to cultivate self-compassion, it's important to understand where our self-criticism comes from. Often, our tendency to be hard on ourselves is deeply ingrained and has roots in our childhood experiences and cultural upbringing. In this chapter, we will explore and understand these roots, so that we can begin to free ourselves from the cycle of self-criticism and develop a more self-compassionate inner voice.

Many of us were raised in environments where perfectionism was highly valued. We were told that only through hard work and a constant striving for excellence could we achieve success and happiness. While there's nothing inherently wrong with wanting to do our best, this mindset often leaves us feeling like we're never good enough, no matter how much we achieve. Our worth becomes tied to our achievements and productivity, and we feel like failures if we fall short of our own or others' expectations.

In addition to societal pressures, our own upbringing can play a role in our self-criticism. If we grew up in an environment where we were constantly criticized or belittled, we may have internalized those messages and now find ourselves being our own worst critic. We may be highly self-critical in order to avoid the pain of being criticized by others, or to protect ourselves from the fear of failure.

The roots of self-criticism can also be traced back to our evolutionary biology. Our brains are wired to be hyper-aware of potential threats and danger, and as a result, we tend to focus on our flaws and shortcomings as a way to protect ourselves from potential rejection or harm. This tendency towards self-criticism can be useful in certain situations, such as when we need to correct a mistake or improve our performance. However, when it becomes a chronic pattern of thinking, it can hold us back and limit our ability to grow and change.

To begin cultivating self-compassion, we must first recognize the patterns of self-criticism in our own lives. This can be a difficult process, as self-criticism often feels like second nature to us. We may not even realize when we're engaging in self-criticism until we start paying closer attention to our thoughts and feelings.

One helpful exercise is to start keeping a journal of our self-talk. When we notice ourselves engaging in self-criticism, we can write down the thought and examine it more closely. Is this thought rooted in reality, or is it an exaggerated or distorted version of the truth? What evidence do we have to support this thought, and what evidence contradicts it? This process of self-inquiry can help us to become more aware of our self-criticism and begin to challenge it.

Another important step is to practice self-compassion in the moment. When we notice ourselves engaging in self-criticism, we can pause and take a few deep breaths, and then remind ourselves that we are only human and that it's okay to make mistakes. We can try to speak to ourselves with the same kindness and understanding that we would offer to a close friend who was struggling.

By exploring and understanding the roots of our self-criticism, and by practicing self-compassion in the moment, we can begin to develop a more self-compassionate inner voice. Over time, this can lead to greater emotional well-being and a more fulfilling life.

19: Cultivating Self-Compassion in Your Relationships

When it comes to relationships, self-compassion can be a powerful tool to increase happiness, improve communication, and build deeper connections. In this chapter, we will explore the ways in which you can cultivate self-compassion within your relationships and experience the many benefits that it has to offer.

The first step in cultivating self-compassion in your relationships is to understand that you are not responsible for other people's emotions. It's easy to fall into the trap of trying to make everyone around you happy, but this is not a realistic goal. Instead, focus on being present and supportive to those around you without sacrificing your own needs.

Next, work on setting healthy boundaries. When we don't have clear boundaries, we can easily fall into patterns of codependency, which can be damaging to both ourselves and our relationships. Set boundaries that protect your time, energy, and emotional well-being, and communicate these boundaries clearly to those around you.

Practicing self-compassion in your relationships also means

allowing yourself to make mistakes. No one is perfect, and everyone makes mistakes. When we can forgive ourselves for our mistakes and move forward, we can create a more compassionate and supportive environment for ourselves and those around us.

Another way to cultivate self-compassion in your relationships is to practice empathy. Empathy involves putting ourselves in someone else's shoes and truly trying to understand their perspective. When we can empathize with others, we can communicate more effectively, resolve conflicts more easily, and create deeper connections.

Finally, remember to take care of yourself. Prioritizing self-care and self-compassion is essential in maintaining healthy relationships. When we are stressed, overworked, or burnt out, it can be difficult to be present and supportive to those around us. Make sure to take time for yourself, engage in activities that bring you joy, and practice self-compassion regularly.

In conclusion, cultivating self-compassion in your relationships can be a powerful way to improve communication, build deeper connections, and increase overall happiness.

19: CULTIVATING SELF-COMPASSION IN YOUR RELA-TIONSHIPS

By setting healthy boundaries, allowing yourself to make mistakes, practicing empathy, and prioritizing self-care, you can create a more compassionate and supportive environment for yourself and those around you.

20: How to Create a Supportive and Compassionate Inner Circle

One of the most crucial elements in creating a fulfilling life is having a supportive and compassionate inner circle. This chapter will guide you through the process of building a community that is both supportive and self-compassionate.

When we have people in our lives who are kind and compassionate, we are more likely to feel loved, accepted, and understood. This, in turn, increases our overall sense of well-being and can help us navigate the difficult times that inevitably come our way.

Here are some tips for creating a supportive and compassionate inner circle:

– Identify Your Needs

The first step to building a supportive and compassionate inner circle is to identify your needs. What do you need from your relationships? Do you need someone to listen to you when you're feeling down? Do you need someone to help you problem-solve? Do you need someone to simply be there for you? Knowing your needs will help you identify the people in your life who are most likely to meet those needs.

– Cultivate a Relationship with Yourself

It is impossible to have healthy and supportive relationships with others if you don't have a healthy relationship with yourself. Spend time getting to know yourself and cultivating self-compassion. When you are able to treat yourself with kindness and compassion, you will be more likely to attract people who do the same.

– Set Boundaries

Setting boundaries is an essential part of building healthy relationships. This means saying "no" when you need to and being clear about what you are and are not willing to tolerate. When you set boundaries, you are communicating your needs and your limits, which will help you build stronger and more supportive relationships.

– Surround Yourself with Like-Minded People

Surround yourself with people who share your values, interests, and goals. These people are more likely to support you and understand your needs. When you have a group of people who share your interests and values, you are more likely to feel supported and understood.

– Be Open to New Relationships

Don't limit yourself to the people you already know. Be open to meeting new people and forming new relationships. This can be as simple as striking up a conversation with someone in line at the grocery store or attending a new social group.

– Practice Compassion in Your Relationships

Once you have identified the people in your life who are supportive and compassionate, it's important to cultivate those relationships. One way to do this is to practice compassion in your interactions with them. Listen to them when they need to talk, support them when they are going through difficult times, and celebrate their successes with them.

– Give as Much as You Receive

Healthy relationships are built on a foundation of mutual giving and receiving. Make sure you are giving as much as you are receiving. This doesn't mean you have to keep a scorecard, but rather that you are putting in effort to support and care for the people in your life.

Building a supportive and compassionate inner circle takes time and effort, but it is well worth it. When you have people in your life who truly care for you and support you, you will be more resilient, happier, and better equipped to handle whatever life throws your way.

21: The Role of Self-Compassion in Self-Care and Well-Being

Self-care is an essential part of our overall well-being, and it involves taking actions that support our physical, emotional, and mental health. However, in our fast-paced world, we often forget to take care of ourselves, and we neglect our own needs. This can lead to stress, burnout, and a sense of feeling overwhelmed. In this chapter, we will explore the role of self-compassion in self-care and well-being.

Self-compassion is an approach to life that emphasizes kindness, understanding, and acceptance toward ourselves. It involves treating ourselves as we would treat a good friend and providing ourselves with the support and care that we need. When we practice self-compassion, we acknowledge our struggles, failures, and mistakes, and we respond with kindness and empathy instead of harsh self-criticism.

Research shows that self-compassion is strongly linked to psychological well-being. People who are more self-compassionate tend to have lower levels of stress, anxiety, and depression. They also have higher levels of happiness, life satisfaction, and resilience. In contrast, people who are more self-critical tend to experience higher levels of stress, anxiety, and depression.

Self-compassion is also closely linked to self-care. When we are self-compassionate, we are more likely to engage in behaviors that support our well-being. For example, we are more likely to exercise regularly, eat healthy foods, get enough sleep, and take breaks when we need them. This is because self-compassion helps us recognize our own needs and respond to them in a supportive and caring way.

Here are some ways to incorporate self-compassion into your self-care routine:

Acknowledge your needs and prioritize self-care. Take the time to identify what you need to feel your best. This may include physical needs like sleep and exercise, emotional needs like connection and support, or mental needs like rest and relaxation. Once you have identified your needs, prioritize them and make time for them in your daily routine.

Treat yourself with kindness and empathy. When you are taking care of yourself, treat yourself with the same kindness and empathy that you would offer to a good friend.

21: THE ROLE OF SELF-COMPASSION IN SELF-CARE AND WELL-BEING

Speak to yourself in a gentle and supportive tone, and offer yourself words of encouragement and comfort.

Practice self-compassion in moments of stress and difficulty. When you are feeling stressed or overwhelmed, take a few deep breaths and offer yourself words of kindness and understanding. Acknowledge that it's normal to feel this way and that you are doing the best you can.

Practice self-compassion in moments of failure or setback. When you experience a setback or failure, it's easy to fall into a spiral of self-criticism and self-blame. Instead, practice self-compassion by acknowledging your feelings and offering yourself words of kindness and support. Remember that failure is a normal part of the learning process, and that you can learn and grow from your mistakes.

Surround yourself with supportive people. Building a supportive network of people who care about you and understand the importance of self-care can be a powerful way to cultivate self-compassion. Seek out people who are positive, encouraging, and understanding, and who support your efforts to take care of yourself.

21: THE ROLE OF SELF-COMPASSION IN SELF-CARE AND WELL-BEING

In conclusion, self-compassion is a powerful tool for self-care and well-being. By treating ourselves with kindness, empathy, and understanding, we can better recognize our own needs and respond to them in a supportive and caring way. Incorporating self-compassion into our daily routines can help us build resilience, reduce stress, and lead a more fulfilling and satisfying life.

22: Creating a Personal Compassion Practice

In order to truly cultivate self-compassion, it's essential to create a personal compassion practice. A personal compassion practice can help you develop and strengthen your self-compassion skills, enabling you to cope with life's challenges with greater ease and resilience.

A personal compassion practice can take many forms, but the core goal is to set aside time each day to engage in activities that help you connect with and care for yourself. This could be something as simple as taking a few minutes each day to offer yourself kind and supportive words, or it could be a more structured practice that incorporates elements of mindfulness, self-reflection, and self-compassion.

To create a personal compassion practice, begin by setting aside time each day to engage in a practice that resonates with you. This could be as little as 5-10 minutes, or it could be as long as an hour or more, depending on your schedule and personal preferences. Some examples of practices you might consider incorporating into your personal compassion practice include:

– Mindful breathing: Take a few moments each day to simply focus on your breath, noticing the sensations of each inhalation and exhalation. This can help you cultivate a greater sense of calm and presence, and can be a helpful way to ground yourself when you're feeling stressed or over-whelmed.

– Loving-kindness meditation: This type of meditation involves silently repeating phrases of kindness and well-wishes to yourself and others. For example, you might say to yourself, "May I be happy, may I be healthy, may I be safe." You can also extend these well-wishes to others, such as loved ones or people you encounter in your day-to-day life.

– Self-reflection: Take time each day to reflect on your thoughts, emotions, and experiences. This can help you develop greater self-awareness, and can be a helpful way to identify patterns of self-criticism or negative self-talk that may be holding you back.

– Gratitude practice: Take a few moments each day to reflect on the things in your life that you're grateful for. This can help you cultivate a greater sense of appreciation and contentment, and can be a helpful way to shift your focus away from negative thoughts or worries.

– Acts of self-care: Incorporate acts of self-care into your daily routine, such as taking a relaxing bath, going for a walk in nature, or reading a book. These activities can help you feel more connected to yourself, and can be a helpful way to replenish your energy and recharge your batteries.

No matter what practices you choose to incorporate into your personal compassion practice, it's important to approach them with an open and non-judgmental attitude. Remember that cultivating self-compassion is a process, and that it's okay to struggle or encounter setbacks along the way. Be patient and kind with yourself, and trust that with time and practice, your self-compassion skills will continue to grow and deepen.

23: Techniques for Practicing Self-Compassion Meditation

Meditation is an effective technique that can help individuals cultivate self-compassion. When individuals practice self-compassion meditation, they learn how to treat themselves with kindness and compassion, even when they are facing difficulties or challenges. This practice can help individuals feel more connected to their emotions, thoughts, and bodies, which can improve their overall well-being and happiness. In this chapter, we will explore various techniques for practicing self-compassion meditation.

– Mindful Breathing

The first technique that we will discuss is mindful breathing. Mindful breathing is a simple and effective technique that can help individuals become more present in the moment. To practice mindful breathing, sit in a comfortable position and focus on your breath. Breathe in slowly through your nose and exhale slowly through your mouth. As you breathe, pay attention to the sensations of the breath moving in and out of your body. If your mind begins to wander, simply bring your attention back to your breath.

23: TECHNIQUES FOR PRACTICING SELF-COMPAS-SION MEDITATION

– Loving-Kindness Meditation

Loving-kindness meditation is a technique that can help individuals develop feelings of warmth and compassion towards themselves and others. To practice loving-kindness meditation, sit in a comfortable position and close your eyes. Focus on your breath for a few moments, and then begin to repeat the following phrases to yourself:

May I be happy.

May I be healthy.

May I be safe.

May I live with ease.

Repeat these phrases for several minutes, imagining that you are sending love and kindness to yourself. Once you feel comfortable with this practice, you can expand it to include other people in your life, imagining that you are sending love and kindness to them as well.

– Body Scan Meditation

Body scan meditation is a technique that can help individuals become more aware of their physical sensations and emotions. To practice body scan meditation, lie down on your back with your arms at your sides and your legs slightly apart. Close your eyes and focus on your breath for a few moments. Then, bring your attention to your toes and notice any sensations in that area. Slowly move your attention up your body, scanning each part of your body and noticing any sensations or emotions that arise.

– Self-Compassion Break

A self-compassion break is a technique that can help individuals cultivate self-compassion in the moment. To practice a self-compassion break, pause for a moment and place your hand on your heart. Take a few deep breaths and say the following phrases to yourself:

This is a moment of suffering.

Suffering is a part of the human experience.

May I be kind to myself in this moment.

Repeat these phrases to yourself a few times, allowing yourself to feel compassion and kindness towards yourself.

– Gratitude Meditation

Gratitude meditation is a technique that can help individuals cultivate feelings of gratitude and appreciation towards themselves and others. To practice gratitude meditation, sit in a comfortable position and close your eyes. Take a few deep breaths and then think about something in your life that you are grateful for. It could be a person, a place, a thing, or even a feeling. Spend a few moments reflecting on this thing and allowing yourself to feel grateful for it.

In conclusion, practicing self-compassion meditation is a powerful way to cultivate self-love, self-kindness, and a more fulfilling life. There are many techniques that individuals can use to practice self-compassion meditation, including mindful breathing, loving-kindness meditation, body scan meditation, self-compassion breaks, and gratitude meditation. By incorporating these techniques into their daily routine, individuals can learn to treat themselves with kindness and compassion, even in challenging moments.

24: Self-Compassionate Breathing Exercises

Breathing exercises are a powerful tool for managing stress and anxiety, and they can also be a powerful way to practice self-compassion. Breathing exercises can help you connect with your body and cultivate a sense of calm and inner peace. By practicing self-compassionate breathing exercises, you can bring a greater sense of kindness and care to yourself in the midst of any challenging experience.

Here are some self-compassionate breathing exercises you can try:

– Abdominal Breathing

Abdominal breathing, also known as diaphragmatic breathing, is a deep breathing technique that can help calm the body and mind. Here's how to do it:

– Find a comfortable, quiet place to sit or lie down.

– Place one hand on your chest and the other on your abdomen.

– Inhale slowly through your nose, letting your abdomen

rise as you fill your lungs with air.

— Exhale slowly through your mouth, letting your abdomen fall as you release the air from your lungs.

— Focus on the rise and fall of your abdomen as you breathe.

— Repeat for several minutes, focusing on your breath and the sensations in your body.

As you breathe, imagine that you are breathing in kindness and compassion for yourself, and breathing out any stress, tension, or self-criticism.

— 4-7-8 Breathing

The 4-7-8 breathing exercise is a simple technique that can help you relax and calm your mind. Here's how to do it:

— Find a comfortable, quiet place to sit or lie down.

— Inhale deeply through your nose for 4 counts.

— Hold your breath for 7 counts.

— Exhale slowly through your mouth for 8 counts.

– Repeat for several minutes, focusing on your breath and the sensations in your body.

As you breathe, imagine that you are breathing in compassion and love for yourself, and breathing out any negative thoughts or emotions.

– Box Breathing

Box breathing is a simple breathing technique that can help calm the body and mind. Here's how to do it:

– Find a comfortable, quiet place to sit or lie down.

– Inhale deeply through your nose for 4 counts.

– Hold your breath for 4 counts.

– Exhale slowly through your mouth for 4 counts.

– Hold your breath for 4 counts.

Repeat for several minutes, focusing on your breath and the sensations in your body.

As you breathe, imagine that you are breathing in compassion and understanding for yourself, and breathing out any tension or stress.

– Loving-Kindness Breathing

Loving-kindness breathing is a practice that can help cultivate feelings of kindness and compassion towards yourself and others. Here's how to do it:

– Find a comfortable, quiet place to sit or lie down.

– Inhale deeply through your nose, imagining that you are breathing in kindness and love for yourself.

– Hold your breath for a few seconds, allowing that feeling of kindness and love to fill your body.

– Exhale slowly through your mouth, imagining that you are breathing out any stress or tension.

Repeat for several minutes, focusing on your breath and the sensations in your body.

As you breathe, imagine that you are sending yourself love, kindness, and compassion with each inhale, and releasing any negative thoughts or emotions with each exhale.

24: SELF-COMPASSIONATE BREATHING EXERCISES

Practicing self-compassionate breathing exercises can help you develop a greater sense of self-awareness and mindfulness, and can help you develop greater self-compassion and self-love. Try incorporating these exercises into your daily routine to help you stay grounded, centered, and connected to your inner wisdom and strength.

25: The Power of Self-Compassionate Journaling

Journaling is an effective tool for practicing self-compassion. Writing about our thoughts, feelings, and experiences can help us understand ourselves better, identify our needs, and connect with our emotions in a non-judgmental way. In this chapter, we'll explore the power of self-compassionate journaling and how to use it to cultivate self-love and find lasting happiness.

Self-compassionate journaling involves writing about our experiences, emotions, and thoughts in a way that is supportive, kind, and non-judgmental. It helps us develop self-awareness, process our emotions, and create a sense of inner peace. Through journaling, we can learn to be more compassionate towards ourselves, acknowledge our strengths, and identify areas where we need to grow.

Here are some techniques for practicing self-compassionate journaling:

– Set the intention: Before you start journaling, take a moment to set an intention for your writing. You might write about a specific issue that's been bothering you or just free-write about whatever comes to mind. Whatever you choose, set an intention to be kind and compassionate towards yourself.

– Practice mindfulness: Bring your attention to the present moment and notice any sensations or emotions that arise. Observe your thoughts without judgment and write about your experience in a non-critical way. If you find yourself judging your thoughts or feelings, try to reframe them in a more positive light.

– Write with self-compassion: When you're writing, imagine that you're talking to a friend who is going through a difficult time. Write in a supportive, kind, and non-judgmental tone, and offer yourself words of encouragement and compassion. Acknowledge your strengths and accomplishments, and recognize the challenges you've overcome.

– Embrace vulnerability: Writing about our vulnerabilities can be difficult, but it's an essential part of cultivating self-compassion. Be honest with yourself about your emotions and experiences, and allow yourself to be vulnerable in your writing. Remember that vulnerability is a sign of strength, not weakness.

25: THE POWER OF SELF-COMPASSIONATE JOURNAL-ING

– Reflect on your progress: As you continue to journal, reflect on your progress and the ways in which you've grown. Celebrate your successes and acknowledge the areas where you still need to work on self-compassion. Use your journal as a tool for self-reflection and self-growth.

Self-compassionate journaling is a powerful tool for cultivating self-love and finding lasting happiness. It allows us to connect with our emotions, acknowledge our strengths and weaknesses, and practice kindness and compassion towards ourselves. Through journaling, we can develop a greater sense of self-awareness and learn to approach ourselves with more kindness and understanding. So pick up a journal and start writing!

26: Using Visualization Techniques to Boost Self-Compassion

Visualization techniques can be a powerful tool in cultivating self-compassion. They allow you to create mental images that represent the kind, nurturing, and supportive voice that you want to develop within yourself.

Here are some visualization exercises that you can try to help you develop greater self-compassion:

– Meeting your future self

Visualize yourself in the future, several years from now, where you have already cultivated self-compassion to a high degree. Imagine your future self as someone who is kind, supportive, and accepting of yourself, flaws and all. Picture yourself talking to your future self, and see them offering you words of kindness, compassion, and wisdom. Think about the advice they might give you to help you on your journey to greater self-compassion.

– Embracing your inner child

Visualize yourself as a child, and imagine that you are hugging and comforting that child. You might picture yourself holding your child-self in your arms, or simply sitting down and talking to them, offering words of kindness, acceptance, and reassurance. Allow yourself to feel the love and compassion that you would naturally feel towards a child, and direct that love towards your inner child-self.

– Developing a self-compassionate inner mentor

Visualize an imaginary figure who represents the kind, compassionate voice that you want to develop within yourself. This might be a spiritual or religious figure, a wise teacher or mentor, or simply an imagined archetype of the wise and nurturing parent or friend. Picture this figure sitting with you, offering words of kindness, comfort, and encouragement. Allow yourself to feel the compassion and support that this figure provides.

– Visualization of a self-compassionate environment

Visualize yourself in a peaceful, supportive environment that represents the qualities of self-compassion that you want to develop within yourself. This might be a natural setting, such as a forest, beach, or mountain, or it could be a cozy and inviting indoor space. Imagine yourself surrounded by beauty, peace, and acceptance, and feel the self-compassion that arises from being in this environment.

Using visualization techniques can be a powerful way to cultivate self-compassion. They allow you to create mental images that represent the kind, nurturing, and supportive voice that you want to develop within yourself. With practice, you can become better at accessing these images, and you may find that they help you to become more self-compassionate in your daily life.

27: The Role of Gratitude in Self-Compassion

Introduction:

Practicing gratitude is an essential aspect of cultivating self-compassion. By expressing gratitude, we can gain a greater appreciation for the present moment, learn to focus on the positive aspects of our lives, and find peace and contentment. In this chapter, we will explore the role of gratitude in self-compassion, its benefits, and various techniques that can help us practice gratitude.

The Importance of Gratitude:

Gratitude is the act of feeling thankful or appreciative for something. It can be as simple as being grateful for the roof over our heads or the food on our table. Practicing gratitude has numerous benefits for our physical and emotional well-being. Here are a few of the reasons why gratitude is essential to self-compassion:

– It helps us focus on the present moment: Gratitude helps us to focus on what we have now and appreciate the present moment rather than worrying about the future or dwelling on the past. By being thankful for the good things in our lives, we can cultivate a sense of peace and contentment.

– It helps us develop a positive outlook: Focusing on what we are grateful for can help us develop a positive outlook on life. When we look for the good in situations, we are less likely to feel overwhelmed or anxious.

– It promotes better relationships: Expressing gratitude can strengthen our relationships with others. By expressing appreciation for others, we can strengthen our bonds and deepen our connections.

Techniques for Practicing Gratitude:

Here are some techniques that can help us cultivate gratitude:

– Gratitude journal: One of the best ways to practice gratitude is to keep a gratitude journal. Each day, take a few minutes to write down three to five things you are grateful for. This can include people, experiences, or even everyday objects. Writing down what we are thankful for can help us appreciate the good in our lives and feel more positive.

– Gratitude letter: Write a letter expressing gratitude to someone who has made a positive impact on your life. This could be a teacher, a family member, a friend, or anyone who has influenced you in a positive way.

– Mindful gratitude practice: This involves taking a moment to pause and reflect on the things we are grateful for. Start by taking a deep breath and bringing to mind something you are grateful for. Allow yourself to really feel the appreciation for that thing or person.

– Gratitude jar: Create a gratitude jar and each day write something you are grateful for on a piece of paper and add it to the jar. At the end of the year, you can read through all of the notes and reflect on the good things that have happened.

The Relationship between Gratitude and Self-Compassion:

Practicing gratitude is an essential aspect of cultivating self-compassion. It helps us to appreciate what we have, focus on the positive aspects of our lives, and feel more positive about ourselves. When we are kind and compassionate to ourselves, we are more likely to be kind and compassionate to others.

27: THE ROLE OF GRATITUDE IN SELF-COMPASSION

Gratitude can also help us to let go of negative emotions and move on from difficult experiences. It can help us to focus on the positive aspects of our lives, rather than dwelling on negative experiences or situations.

Conclusion:

Gratitude is an essential component of self-compassion. It helps us to appreciate what we have, focus on the positive aspects of our lives, and feel more positive about ourselves. By cultivating gratitude, we can learn to let go of negative emotions, develop a positive outlook, and strengthen our relationships with others. By incorporating gratitude into our daily lives, we can reap the benefits of a more positive and fulfilling life.

28: How to Overcome Self-Sabotage with Self-Compassion

Self-sabotage is a common problem that many people face at some point in their lives. It involves engaging in behaviors that are harmful or counterproductive to our well-being, despite our conscious desire to achieve our goals. This can include things like procrastination, self-doubt, and self-criticism.

If you find yourself engaging in self-sabotage, it is important to address this behavior with self-compassion. Self-compassion can help you understand the underlying reasons for your self-sabotage and develop the tools to overcome it.

The first step in overcoming self-sabotage is to identify the behaviors that are holding you back. This can be challenging, as self-sabotage often operates at an unconscious level. It may be helpful to keep a journal or use a self-assessment tool to gain a better understanding of your patterns.

Once you have identified your self-sabotaging behaviors, it is important to approach them with a sense of self-compassion. This means acknowledging that these behaviors are not a reflection of your worth as a person and recognizing that everyone has struggles and challenges in life.

One way to develop self-compassion is to practice self-forgiveness. This means accepting that you are human and that making mistakes is a normal part of the human experience. By forgiving yourself for your past mistakes, you can let go of any feelings of guilt or shame that may be contributing to your self-sabotaging behaviors.

Another way to cultivate self-compassion is to practice self-kindness. This means treating yourself with the same kindness and care that you would offer to a close friend. Instead of criticizing yourself for your mistakes, try offering yourself words of encouragement and support.

In addition to self-compassion, there are several practical steps you can take to overcome self-sabotage. One effective technique is to break your goals down into smaller, more manageable steps. This can help you avoid feeling overwhelmed and discouraged, which can lead to self-sabotaging behaviors.

28: HOW TO OVERCOME SELF-SABOTAGE WITH SELF-COMPASSION

It can also be helpful to seek support from others. This might involve working with a therapist or coach who can help you identify and overcome your self-sabotaging behaviors. Alternatively, you might find it helpful to join a support group or talk to a trusted friend or family member about your struggles.

Finally, it is important to stay motivated and committed to your goals. This means cultivating a sense of purpose and passion for the things that you want to achieve. By focusing on your goals and staying motivated, you can overcome your self-sabotaging behaviors and achieve the success and happiness that you deserve.

In conclusion, self-sabotage can be a challenging and frustrating problem to overcome, but it is possible with the help of self-compassion and practical techniques. By approaching your self-sabotaging behaviors with self-compassion, breaking your goals down into manageable steps, seeking support from others, and staying motivated and committed, you can overcome your self-sabotage and create a more fulfilling and satisfying life.

29: Practicing Self-Compassion in the Workplace

In today's fast-paced world, the workplace can often feel like a highly competitive environment. As a result, it can be easy to fall into a pattern of self-criticism, perfectionism, and overworking. However, these patterns can be detrimental to our well-being and ultimately reduce our productivity in the long run. Cultivating self-compassion in the workplace is a vital tool for thriving in a fast-paced and competitive environment.

Self-compassion involves treating oneself with kindness, care, and understanding, even in the face of failure, mistakes, or imperfections. Practicing self-compassion in the workplace can help reduce stress, boost creativity, and increase job satisfaction. Here are some techniques for practicing self-compassion in the workplace:

– Practice mindfulness: Mindfulness involves being fully present and aware of the present moment without judgment. Practicing mindfulness at work can help you stay focused, calm, and centered, even during stressful situations. Take a few moments each day to practice mindfulness, whether it be through breathing exercises, meditation, or mindful walking.

– Set realistic goals: Setting overly ambitious goals or having unrealistic expectations of oneself can lead to feelings of failure, disappointment, and burnout. Setting realistic goals that align with your values, strengths, and limitations can help you achieve more and feel a sense of accomplishment without sacrificing your well-being.

– Celebrate small wins: Celebrating small wins can help build momentum, increase motivation, and foster a sense of accomplishment. Take a moment to acknowledge and celebrate your accomplishments, no matter how small they may seem.

– Use positive self-talk: The way we talk to ourselves can greatly influence our mood, behavior, and overall well-being. Instead of berating yourself for mistakes or shortcomings, practice using positive and encouraging self-talk. Use phrases such as "I am doing the best I can," "I am capable of handling this situation," and "I am proud of myself for trying."

– Practice self-care: Taking care of yourself is essential for thriving in the workplace. Make sure to prioritize self-care by getting enough sleep, eating nutritious foods, staying hydrated, and engaging in physical activity. These activities can help boost your energy, productivity, and overall well-being.

– Seek support: Seeking support from colleagues, mentors, or a professional can be a valuable resource for practicing self-compassion in the workplace. Having a supportive network can help reduce stress, provide new perspectives, and foster a sense of community.

In conclusion, practicing self-compassion in the workplace is an essential tool for thriving in a fast-paced and competitive environment. By incorporating mindfulness, setting realistic goals, celebrating small wins, using positive self-talk, practicing self-care, and seeking support, you can cultivate self-compassion and ultimately achieve greater well-being and success in the workplace.

30: The Connection Between Self-Compassion and Creativity

As human beings, we are all inherently creative. We have the capacity to innovate, problem-solve, and create art in various forms. However, many of us may find that our creativity gets stifled from time to time, and we may feel stuck or unproductive. This is where self-compassion comes in. In this chapter, we will explore the connection between self-compassion and creativity, and how cultivating self-compassion can help us unlock our creative potential.

Self-compassion is an attitude of kindness, non-judgment, and mindfulness towards oneself. When we are self-compassionate, we are able to acknowledge our mistakes and failures without judgment, and we treat ourselves with the same care and compassion that we would offer to a good friend. Self-compassion allows us to accept our imperfections and limitations, and it helps us to stay motivated and resilient in the face of setbacks and challenges.

There are several ways in which self-compassion can enhance our creativity. Firstly, when we are self-compassionate, we are less likely to engage in self-criticism or self-doubt, which can be major barriers to creativity. Self-criticism can create a negative feedback loop that can stifle our creative process, while self-doubt can prevent us from taking risks and trying new things. When we approach our creative endeavors with self-compassion, we are more likely to have a growth mindset and be open to experimentation and learning.

Secondly, self-compassion can help us to overcome the fear of failure that often accompanies creativity. When we are self-compassionate, we are able to recognize that failure is a natural part of the creative process, and we can view our failures as opportunities for growth and learning rather than as personal flaws or shortcomings. This mindset allows us to take risks and pursue our creative passions with a greater sense of ease and freedom.

Thirdly, self-compassion can help us to access the deeper parts of ourselves that are often the source of our creativity. When we are self-compassionate, we are able to connect with our emotions and vulnerabilities in a way that can inspire and inform our creative work. We are also able to tap into our intuition and trust our inner voice, which can lead to more authentic and original creative expressions.

30: THE CONNECTION BETWEEN SELF-COMPASSION AND CREATIVITY

So, how can we cultivate self-compassion in our creative endeavors? One way is to practice self-compassion meditation or journaling, as discussed in previous chapters. Another way is to use affirmations or mantras that promote self-compassion and creativity. For example, you could repeat the phrase "I am creative and deserving of self-compassion" to yourself when you feel self-doubt or creative blockages.

It's also important to make time for self-care and self-nurturing activities that support our creativity. This could include taking breaks from our work, engaging in hobbies or activities that we enjoy, or spending time in nature. When we prioritize our own well-being and self-compassion, we create the space and energy that is necessary for creativity to flourish.

In conclusion, self-compassion is a powerful tool for unlocking our creative potential. By approaching our creative endeavors with kindness, non-judgment, and mindfulness, we can overcome self-criticism, fear of failure, and other barriers that can stifle our creativity. When we prioritize our own self-compassion and self-care, we create the conditions for our creativity to thrive, and we are able to express

ourselves in more authentic, meaningful, and fulfilling
ways.

31: Exploring the Spiritual Dimension of Self-Compassion

Self-compassion is often thought of in psychological and emotional terms, but it can also have a spiritual dimension. Many spiritual traditions emphasize compassion and kindness toward oneself and others as an important part of a fulfilled life. In this chapter, we will explore the relationship between self-compassion and spirituality and how to cultivate self-compassion from a spiritual perspective.

One way to approach self-compassion from a spiritual perspective is to consider the interconnectedness of all beings. In many spiritual traditions, the idea that all beings are connected is fundamental. This interconnectedness can be seen as a source of compassion, as our actions impact others in ways we may not even realize. By recognizing this interconnectedness, we can cultivate greater compassion for ourselves and for others.

Another important aspect of self-compassion in a spiritual context is the practice of forgiveness. Forgiveness is often seen as a key component of many spiritual practices, and self-forgiveness is a crucial part of self-compassion. When we hold onto self-blame and self-judgment, we create unnecessary suffering for ourselves. Forgiving ourselves for past mistakes or shortcomings can be a powerful way to cultivate self-compassion.

Meditation and prayer can also be helpful tools in cultivating self-compassion from a spiritual perspective. Taking time to connect with a higher power or inner wisdom can help us access a deeper sense of compassion and kindness toward ourselves. This can also help us tap into our own inner strength and resilience, which can be useful in navigating difficult times.

In some spiritual traditions, self-compassion is seen as a natural outgrowth of a deeper sense of compassion for all beings. When we cultivate compassion for others, it naturally spills over into how we treat ourselves. This is sometimes referred to as "enlightened self-interest" - by taking care of ourselves with kindness and compassion, we are better equipped to show up for others with the same qualities.

One potential challenge in exploring the spiritual dimension of self-compassion is that it can be difficult to separate from religious or cultural beliefs. It is important to remember that self-compassion is a personal practice that can be approached from a variety of perspectives. It is possible to cultivate self-compassion without subscribing to a specific spiritual tradition or belief system.

Here are some practical ways to cultivate self-compassion from a spiritual perspective:

– Engage in meditation or prayer to connect with a higher power or inner wisdom. This can help cultivate a deeper sense of compassion and kindness toward ourselves.

– Practice forgiveness, both of ourselves and others. This can be a powerful way to release self-blame and judgment and cultivate self-compassion.

– Cultivate an awareness of interconnectedness. Recognize that our actions impact others and that compassion for ourselves and others is interconnected.

– Use self-compassion as a tool for social justice. Recognize the ways in which societal structures and systems impact individuals and use self-compassion to stay engaged in the work of creating a more just and equitable world.

– Take time for self-care and self-nurturing activities. This can help us build resilience and better show up for ourselves and others.

In summary, self-compassion can have a spiritual dimension that is often overlooked in traditional discussions of the topic. Cultivating compassion and kindness for oneself can be a powerful way to connect with a deeper sense of interconnectedness and higher purpose. By using meditation, forgiveness, and other spiritual practices, we can cultivate self-compassion from a spiritual perspective and live a more fulfilled life.

32: Integrating Self-Compassion into Your Daily Life

Introduction:

In this chapter, we will explore how to integrate self-compassion into your daily life. While many people may be able to practice self-compassion in moments of distress or during specific activities, it can be challenging to make self-compassion a consistent part of our daily routine. However, by making a conscious effort to integrate self-compassion into our daily lives, we can experience the many benefits of this practice on a more consistent basis.

The Importance of Integrating Self-Compassion into Your Daily Life:

Integrating self-compassion into your daily life has numerous benefits. It can help to reduce stress, anxiety, and depression while increasing feelings of well-being and happiness. When we practice self-compassion regularly, it becomes a habit, and we are more likely to show ourselves kindness and understanding even in difficult situations.

Techniques for Integrating Self-Compassion into Your Daily

32: INTEGRATING SELF-COMPASSION INTO YOUR DAILY LIFE

Life:

— Set an intention for the day:

One way to integrate self-compassion into your daily life is by setting an intention for the day. This can be done first thing in the morning before you get out of bed or at any point during the day when you feel you need a reset. Setting an intention can help you to focus on the positive and can serve as a reminder to be kind to yourself throughout the day.

— Practice mindfulness:

Mindfulness is a powerful tool for cultivating self-compassion. When we practice mindfulness, we become more aware of our thoughts and feelings without judgment. We can observe our emotions without getting caught up in them or allowing them to control our actions. This can help us to respond to ourselves with more kindness and understanding.

— Take breaks throughout the day:

Taking breaks throughout the day is essential for maintaining your well-being. It can help you to manage stress, reduce fatigue, and boost your overall productivity. During your breaks, take time to do something you enjoy, such as reading a book, going for a walk, or practicing a hobby. Taking these moments to nurture yourself is an act of self-compassion.

– Practice self-care:

Self-care is an essential aspect of self-compassion. Taking care of yourself physically, emotionally, and mentally is critical for your overall well-being. Make sure to prioritize your self-care needs by eating well, getting enough sleep, engaging in physical activity, and taking time for relaxation and reflection.

– Cultivate a self-compassion mantra:

A self-compassion mantra can help you to remember to be kind and understanding towards yourself throughout the day. Choose a phrase or affirmation that resonates with you, such as "I am doing the best I can," or "I am worthy of love and compassion." Repeat this mantra to yourself throughout the day as a reminder of your commitment to self-compassion.

– Surround yourself with supportive people:

Surrounding yourself with people who support your self-compassion practice can be helpful. Having friends, family, or colleagues who encourage you to be kind to yourself can provide a positive influence and can help you to stay on track with your self-compassion goals.

Conclusion:

Integrating self-compassion into your daily life requires a conscious effort, but the benefits are well worth it. By setting intentions, practicing mindfulness, taking breaks, prioritizing self-care, cultivating a self-compassion mantra, and surrounding yourself with supportive people, you can make self-compassion a consistent part of your life. Remember, self-compassion is not a one-time event or a quick fix. It is a practice that requires patience, dedication, and a commitment to yourself. By making self-compassion a priority, you can unlock the power of self-love and find lasting happiness in your daily life.

33: Maintaining Self-Compassion in the Face of Setbacks and Challenges

Self-compassion can be an excellent tool for managing the difficult times in life, such as setbacks and challenges. When we encounter these obstacles, it can be easy to slip into negative self-talk and self-blame. However, cultivating self-compassion can help us respond to these difficulties in a more positive and constructive way.

In this chapter, we will explore how to maintain self-compassion during setbacks and challenges. We will cover several techniques and strategies that can help you stay grounded, resilient, and self-compassionate when facing adversity.

Recognize and Accept the Struggle

The first step to maintaining self-compassion during setbacks and challenges is to recognize and accept that you are struggling. This may sound obvious, but many people try to deny or suppress their negative feelings when they encounter obstacles. This can be counterproductive because it can lead to feelings of shame, inadequacy, and isolation.

Instead, try to recognize and accept the struggle as a normal part of the human experience. Acknowledge that everyone faces challenges, setbacks, and failures. Allow yourself to feel whatever emotions come up, whether it is disappointment, frustration, anger, or sadness.

Self-compassion involves treating ourselves with the same kindness and understanding that we would offer to a close friend who is struggling. So, imagine how you would respond to a friend who is going through a tough time. Would you criticize them, blame them, or tell them to suck it up? Or would you offer them support, empathy, and encouragement? Use this same approach with yourself.

Practice Mindfulness

Mindfulness is the practice of being present in the moment, observing our thoughts and feelings without judgment. Mindfulness can help us stay grounded and calm during difficult times by enabling us to recognize our emotions without becoming overwhelmed by them.

One of the simplest mindfulness practices is mindful breathing. Find a quiet place where you won't be disturbed, sit down, and focus on your breath. Inhale deeply through your nose and exhale slowly through your mouth. As you breathe, focus your attention on the sensation of the air moving in and out of your body. If your mind starts to wander, gently bring it back to your breath.

You can also practice mindfulness while doing everyday activities, such as washing the dishes, walking, or even eating. Focus your attention on the sensations of the activity and try to stay present in the moment. This can help you stay centered and focused during challenging situations.

Reframe Your Thoughts

One of the most significant obstacles to maintaining self-compassion during setbacks and challenges is negative self-talk. When we encounter difficulties, our inner critic can become activated, leading to self-blame, self-doubt, and self-criticism. This can be damaging to our self-esteem and self-worth.

To counteract negative self-talk, it can be helpful to reframe our thoughts in a more positive and constructive way. For example, instead of telling yourself, "I'm such a failure," try to reframe your thoughts as, "I'm disappointed that this didn't work out, but I can learn from this experience and try again." This can help you maintain a growth mindset and see setbacks as opportunities for growth and learning.

Practice Self-Care

During times of stress and difficulty, it is essential to take care of yourself. Self-care involves taking deliberate actions to nurture your physical, mental, and emotional well-being. This can include activities such as exercise, getting enough sleep, eating healthy, and engaging in activities that bring you joy.

Practicing self-care can help you maintain your resilience and mental fortitude during challenging times. It can also be an act of self-compassion, demonstrating to yourself that you

34: Self-Compassion as a Path to Inner Healing and Growth

Self-compassion is not just about feeling better in the moment; it's about creating a foundation for growth and healing. By learning to treat ourselves with kindness and understanding, we create a safe space for personal transformation and development. In this chapter, we'll explore how self-compassion can serve as a path to inner healing and growth.

Healing is a process that involves recognizing and attending to our emotional wounds. It's about giving ourselves the time and space to grieve, reflect, and come to terms with the challenges we've faced in life. Self-compassion can help us to do this in a gentle and supportive way. By offering ourselves the same kindness, care, and concern we would offer to a dear friend, we create a safe space for our emotional wounds to be acknowledged and healed.

The first step in using self-compassion as a path to healing and growth is to become aware of our emotional struggles. This requires tuning into our inner world and acknowledging the pain and suffering we're experiencing. We can do this through mindfulness practices, such as meditation or deep breathing, which help us to become more aware of our thoughts and emotions.

Once we've become aware of our emotional struggles, we can begin to offer ourselves self-compassion. This involves treating ourselves with the same kindness, care, and concern we would offer to a dear friend. We can do this by using the self-compassion practices we've learned throughout this book, such as self-compassionate journaling or visualization.

Self-compassion can also help us to reframe our experiences in a more positive light. When we're faced with setbacks or challenges, it's easy to become stuck in a negative cycle of self-blame and self-criticism. However, by approaching ourselves with self-compassion, we can begin to see our experiences in a more positive light. We can recognize that our struggles are a natural part of the human experience, and that we're not alone in our suffering.

By approaching ourselves with kindness and understanding, we create a space for personal growth and development. Self-compassion allows us to explore our emotional wounds with curiosity and compassion, rather than judgment and criticism. This allows us to learn from our experiences, and to develop a greater sense of self-awareness and insight.

In addition to personal growth and development, self-compassion can also help us to develop deeper connections with others. When we're able to treat ourselves with kindness and understanding, we become more attuned to the needs of others. We're better able to empathize with their struggles, and to offer them the same kindness and care we offer ourselves.

In order to maintain self-compassion as a path to inner healing and growth, it's important to cultivate a regular practice. This can involve setting aside time each day for self-compassionate practices such as meditation, visualization, or journaling. It can also involve incorporating self-compassion into our daily routines, such as taking a self-compassionate break during a busy day, or offering ourselves kind and supportive self-talk when we're feeling overwhelmed.

In conclusion, self-compassion can serve as a powerful path to inner healing and growth. By treating ourselves with kindness and understanding, we create a safe space for our emotional wounds to be acknowledged and healed. This allows us to develop a deeper sense of self-awareness and insight, and to cultivate deeper connections with others. To maintain self-compassion as a path to growth and healing, it's important to cultivate a regular practice, and to approach ourselves with kindness and understanding in all areas of our lives.

35: Overcoming Barriers to Self-Compassion

Despite the many benefits of self-compassion, some people still struggle to develop and maintain this skill. There are many reasons why this might be the case. For example, some people may have grown up in environments where self-criticism was the norm, while others may fear that being kind to themselves will make them lazy or complacent. In this chapter, we will explore some common barriers to self-compassion and offer tips and strategies for overcoming them.

– Self-Criticism

Self-criticism is one of the main barriers to self-compassion. If you are used to being hard on yourself, it can be difficult to suddenly switch to a more compassionate mindset. One strategy for overcoming self-criticism is to start by simply noticing when you are being self-critical. Try to observe your thoughts without judgment and ask yourself if you would speak to a friend in the same way. Another technique is to try to reframe your negative self-talk. For example, instead of saying "I'm such an idiot for forgetting my keys," try saying "I made a mistake, but that doesn't mean I'm a bad person."

– Fear of Being Self-Indulgent

Some people worry that practicing self-compassion will make them lazy or self-indulgent. They fear that if they let themselves off the hook too easily, they will never achieve anything. However, research has shown that self-compassion is actually associated with greater motivation and resilience. When we treat ourselves with kindness, we are more likely to bounce back from setbacks and to take on challenges with greater confidence. If you find yourself struggling with this barrier, try to reframe your thinking. Remember that self-compassion is not the same as self-pity or self-indulgence. It is simply a way of treating yourself with the same kindness and understanding that you would offer to a good friend.

– Guilt and Shame

Guilt and shame can also be significant barriers to self-compassion. If you feel guilty or ashamed about something you have done, it can be hard to show yourself kindness and understanding. However, it is important to remember that everyone makes mistakes and that we all have things we regret. When we can accept our imperfections and forgive ourselves for our mistakes, we can move forward with greater ease and clarity. To overcome this barrier, try to practice self-forgiveness. Recognize that you are human and that you are not perfect. Offer yourself the same kindness and understanding that you would offer to a friend who was struggling with similar feelings.

– Fear of Vulnerability

Many people are afraid to show vulnerability and to let others see their softer side. They worry that if they are too kind to themselves, they will be seen as weak or needy. However, vulnerability is actually a strength, not a weakness. When we can be vulnerable and show our true selves, we create deeper connections with others and are better able to cultivate meaningful relationships. To overcome this barrier, try to practice self-compassion in small ways, such as offering yourself a kind word or doing something nice for yourself. As you become more comfortable with this practice, you may find that you are better able to show vulnerability in other areas of your life.

– Lack of Time

Finally, many people feel that they simply don't have enough time to practice self-compassion. They may be busy with work, family, or other responsibilities and feel that self-care is a luxury they can't afford. However, taking care of yourself is not a luxury, it is a necessity. When we are kind to ourselves and take time to recharge, we are better able to show up for others and to do our best work.

36: Conclusion: A Future Filled with Self-Compassion and Happiness

Congratulations! You have come to the end of this self-compassion guide, and I hope you have found it to be a valuable resource on your journey toward greater happiness, well-being, and self-love.

Throughout this book, we have explored the power of self-compassion as a tool for overcoming negative self-talk, self-criticism, and self-doubt, and for cultivating a sense of inner peace and acceptance. We have also looked at the many benefits of self-compassion, from reduced stress and anxiety to improved relationships and increased resilience in the face of life's challenges.

However, as you know, self-compassion is not a destination, but rather a journey. It takes time and effort to develop this quality within ourselves, and setbacks are inevitable. But with practice, we can cultivate a mindset of self-compassion that will carry us through even the toughest times.

In this final chapter, we will review some key takeaways from this book and provide you with some tips for continu-

ing your self-compassion practice long after you have fin-
ished reading.

Key Takeaways:

– Self-compassion is the practice of treating ourselves with
the same kindness, concern, and understanding that we
would offer to a dear friend.

– There are three core components of self-compassion: self-
kindness, common humanity, and mindfulness. These components work together to create a sense of warmth, connection, and presence within ourselves.

– Self-compassion has numerous benefits for our mental
and physical health, including reducing stress, anxiety, and
depression, increasing resilience, and improving our relationships.

– Self-compassion is not the same as self-indulgence, self-
pity, or self-esteem. Rather, it is a way of responding to our
own suffering with empathy and support, rather than criticism or judgment.

– There are many practices that can help us develop self-compassion, such as self-compassionate journaling, meditation, self-compassionate breathing, visualization, gratitude, and more.

Tips for Continuing Your Self-Compassion Practice:

− Practice self-compassion regularly. Just like any other skill, self-compassion requires consistent practice to become a habit. Set aside some time each day for self-compassion practices that work for you.

− Be patient with yourself. Developing self-compassion takes time and effort, and you may experience setbacks along the way. Treat yourself with kindness and compassion as you work through these challenges.

− Seek support. Sometimes it can be difficult to practice self-compassion on our own. Consider joining a support group, working with a therapist, or talking to friends and family who understand and support your goals.

− Celebrate your successes. Recognize the progress you have made in your self-compassion practice, no matter how small. Celebrate your successes and use them as motivation

36: CONCLUSION: A FUTURE FILLED WITH SELF-COM-PASSION AND HAPPINESS

to continue on your path.

– Remember your motivation. Keep in mind why you started practicing self-compassion in the first place. What benefits are you hoping to gain? What changes do you want to see in your life? Remind yourself of these goals when you feel discouraged or stuck.

In conclusion, self-compassion is a powerful tool for transforming our relationship with ourselves and with the world around us. It allows us to embrace our imperfections and challenges with a sense of empathy and kindness, and to view our struggles as part of the shared human experience. As we continue to cultivate self-compassion, we open the door to greater happiness, peace, and fulfillment in our lives. I wish you all the best on your self-compassion journey, and I hope this

Thank You

As we reach the end of this book, I want to say thanks for reading this book.

I want to get this information out to as many people as possible. If you found this book helpful, I would greatly appreciate you leaving me a review. This helps others find the book as well.

Disclaimer

This document is geared towards providing exact and reliable information in regards to the topic and issue covered. The publication is sold on the idea that the publisher is not required to render an accounting, officially permitted, or otherwise, qualified services. If advice is necessary, legal, financial, medical or professional, a practiced individual in the profession should be ordered.

This information is not presented by a financial or medical practitioner and is for entertainment, educational and informational purposes only. The content is not intended as a substitute for professional medical advice, diagnosis, or treatment. Always seek the advice of your physician or other qualified health care provider with any questions you may have regarding a medical condition. Never disregard professional medical advice or delay in seeking it because of something you have read.

The information provided herein is stated to be truthful and consistent, in that any liability, in terms of inattention or otherwise, by any usage or abuse of any policies, processes, or directions contained within is the solitary and utter responsibility of the recipient reader. Under no circumstances

DISCLAIMER

will any legal responsibility or blame be held against the publisher for any reparation, damages, or monetary loss due to the information herein, either directly or indirectly.

www.ingramcontent.com/pod-product-compliance
Lightning Source LLC
Chambersburg PA
CBHW060540130626
46553CB00002B/838